El Dorado

PETER CAMPION

El Dorado

THE UNIVERSITY OF CHICAGO PRESS

Chicago & London

PETER CAMPION teaches in the MFA program at the University of
Minnesota. He is the author of two previous collections of poems, *Other
People* and *The Lions*, both published by the University of Chicago Press.

The University of Chicago Press, Chicago 60637
The University of Chicago Press, Ltd., London
© 2013 by The University of Chicago
All rights reserved. Published 2013.
Printed in the United States of America
22 21 20 19 18 17 16 15 14 13   1 2 3 4 5

ISBN-13: 978-0-226-07711-6 (paper)
ISBN-13: 978-0-226-07725-3 (e-book)
DOI: 10.7208/chicago/9780226077253.001.0001

Library of Congress Cataloging-in-Publication Data
Campion, Peter, 1976– author.
    [Poems. Selections]
    El Dorado / Peter Campion.
        pages cm. — (Phoenix poets)
    Includes bibliographical references.
    Poems.
    ISBN 978-0-226-07711-6 (paperback : alkaline paper) —
    ISBN 978-0-226-07725-3 (e-book)
    I. Title. II. Series: Phoenix poets.
    PS3603.A486A6 2013
    811'.6—dc23

                            2013017716

♾ This paper meets the requirements of ANSI/NISO Z39.48-1992
(Permanence of Paper).

for Amy, Jack, and Lizzie

Should you ever be athirst in the great American desert, try this experiment.

CONTENTS

ACKNOWLEDGMENTS

Thanks to the editors of the following journals in which these poems were first published:

AGNI: "Rome"
At Length: "Salt Water (III)," "Elegy with Television"
Columbia Journal: "Danielle," "Villa Sciarra: Azaleas"
Congeries (Connotations Press): "Primitive Figure, Dogu Period"
    (as "Blue Figure, Dogu Period")
The Cortland Review: "Securities"
Diode: "Blood Brook," "Salt Water (I)"
Free Verse: "Chicago: The Congress Plaza"
Harvard Review: "1986: The Court"
The Kenyon Review: "Letter from Ohio"
The New Republic: "Vermont: Gile Mountain"
The Ocean State Review: "After Baudelaire: I Have Not Forgotten . . ."
Poetry: "Dandelions," "Over Greenland: Flight 107"
Provincetown Arts: "Los Angeles River"
Redivider: "Salt Water (II)," "1995: The Sawtooths"
Slate: "Salt Water (IV)," "El Dorado"
Threepenny Review: "Car Radio Near Cleveland Near Dawn"

"Salt Water (I)" also appeared in the *Alhambra Poetry Calendar, 2010*.
"1986: The Court" appeared on *Poetry Daily* (poems.com).

Gratitude to the American Academy of Arts and Letters, the Drue Heinz Trust, and the American Academy in Rome for the gift of a Joseph Brodsky Rome Prize Fellowship.

Thanks as well to the John Simon Guggenheim Memorial Foundation for the time and support provided by a Fellowship in Creative Arts.

El Dorado

EL DORADO

After the accident when we were
safe on the shoulder and she leaned against me
gripping our son as the cruiser
strobed blue and red

there came the helplessness   the bare
nerve shudder giving up to air

so in those moments
"I" was this person with my name and also no one

so remembering
                    crumpled steel and
sun on the silos for miles beyond us

I can make no connection

———

Only the ancient story   how a man
clambered from caves where days he dwelt alone
and tribesmen came anointing him
with balsam gum then
sputtering gold dust
through wooden tubes all over him

He walked the talus to the lake where a raft awaited
braziers lavishing shine on the heaped gold

At the center of the lake he scattered
handfuls of gold to the water
and returning to the shore
he doused himself
so colors elusive as the coins and squiggles
on the dorsal of a trout

fell to the cratered basin   treasure
the invaders found
vanishing always to wild interior

fell as the tribesmen
bellowed through jaguar masks

—

No one along the breakdown lane in northern Iowa
dressed as a jaguar

No one dripped with gold

But that shiver of surrender
flooding my chest
               that tremble of unclenching muscle

stranded in the miles of soybean fields
between one home we left and one we'd never seen

I tell you   my wife and son
their warmth against me
                        the houses
small from the road as a spatter of paint chips

even the billboard above us   chewed up
furniture bobbing in the blue
                                even my own skin

shone with the promise
there was nothing more than this
train of moments

streaming through air
                        everything gathering
light to its contours
before it disappears

SECURITIES

Beyond my father's distance and beyond his father's.
Back a century. My great grandfather's desk
in Cincinnati. How he must have cherished
its distance from the power looms below
and must have known: the fierce
precision of his nib on the accounts
pinning him down as sun
leaked orange across the river
kept him from falling
back there
                    and kept his wife
if this year she was
                        home from the sanatorium
afloat in her complete
edition of Browning
                    (which I own)
and kept his children
bound to the education that would carry them
thank God away from there.

The desk. It must have been a rolltop.
Maple with locking drawers and blotter.
Ribbon of accounting tape. Ledgers in which
the loops and slashes must have borne
even through Palmer Method regularity
his own peculiar animal impress.

But across such distance
                    so much "must have been."

This morning
                    wrestling my son
I kiss his chest then trumpet a tickling fart noise
until he wriggles free
                    and shouts "again."

What aristocratic privilege
to squirm in bed like this.
What sweet barbaric closeness of our skin.

What solace and uneasiness
to know: however long from now
however distant in the loom of
office towers
                    underwater green at night
and wing lights on cargo planes
and glimmer from the squatter shacks
under an overpass

one memory of nerves
tensed then released to
                    warmth in his ribcage
will flow from this.

And then what solace and uneasiness

not to know
and only to press my face to him again.

BOSTON: RED HAIR

Up from subway stairs

ringlets and cleavage
slick with glitter paste she used

to advertise down Washington
down Tremont and that city

we were born in
swiping her consonants:

"hey Peetah got a light?"

My warmest "oh so good to see . . ."
while groping pockets

(she knew) was a lie

and this betrayal miniscule
but absolute.

Pity
        the lowest currency how many
husbands and fathers must have paid before
coming inside her.

"How does a girl like you?"

But oh
        our Saint Paul's Sunday school

our lips orange smeared with alphabet soup.

Maureen
        oh more than I can hold
in my mouth.

You swatted your hand to mean
some small forgiveness

or none

before you disappeared again
inside the wide

electrical fire.

CONCOURSE C
after the Exeter Book, *Riddles of the Wind*

Frequency-hopping spectrum spreads
that cell-phone gabble rides.

And microbes.

And MPEG compression signals
buzzing the news.

Incredible to picture
all that invisible
swirl of the concourse.

Some stranger sidles up
and spits to his headset:
                    "Bob is such bullshit.
He tells me standard chassis, standard chassis.

Where's his order though? Our ass is getting
reamed in the Carolinas.

Florida too.

Hello? Hello? Can you put Helen through?"

Beside him, phosphorescent palm to ear

as she gingerly dabs mascara:
"I was like
             the silence tells me

you have issues with dependency.
But he was like
             you turn it all emotional."

Spliced with CNN's "subprime lenders
Peshawar car bomb"

the words unfasten:

free from their meanings and sources
as smells of coffee or Givenchy.

High on the plate glass
an ashen roil
pulsed by lightning

lingers above the hangars.

Fused with the rush
(this sheer American everything jammed at once)

the storm could be a signal
gathering up all others cramming air
with their binary streams:

its voice some ancient soothsayer's
riddling glottals and plosives:

"Who is so smart
that he can tell who drives my outcast force

when I arise along fate's road in wrath

and, groaning so grandly, spume down my power
on forests and village homes

cracking their rafters as I plunder?

Smoke and ash plume out and cries of the dying.

Then in the woodlands
I splinter flowering branches and slash down
trees as I wander (water for my roof)

this path enclosed by . . . whose enclosing power?

The rains that spin from me
once wrapped the flesh and souls of men.

So say who shrouds my force.
Say who I am.
                        Who makes me bear this hurt?"

Static.

The heat lamp glow from Sbarro
and Popeye's Chicken.

Runway lights awash
                         though lines keep boarding.

And the crowd still
rises on escalators from the train

as the news feed returns
to burning tires and
                         (cordoned off)
a woman's mute howls.

Whatever force propels us
shows its true desires
                         (monstrous, innocent)

only through narrow bands.

The way that no one dares
stare at the soldier
                         late for boarding
off to the corner

hefting his toddler son.

Or those voices that disclose themselves
naked for moments in the digital rain:

"Sometimes I ride the clouds that ride my back
and spill their water
                         all across the earth.

And sometimes I collide them.
Metal on metal's

no louder when they lash against each other
shedding their angled flames.

Bare terror fills
whole townships as the battle gleams and bellows.

Only a dullard never fears the arrow.

He dies regardless when my leader flies
down through the rain to loose his fire-shower."

Static again.

"I know he loves me, but . . ."

"Hello? Hello? Can you put Helen through?"

14

DANIELLE

Broadcast all down the Shenandoah Valley
Reverend Billy shouts "surrender
to the love of Jesus Christ will get you there."
His drawl a stream
beneath the words
                    floating the words
his voice goes streaky as the sun
slashing through sumac.

Yammer from Watkins Glen:
"Juan Pablo on the rumble strips
and Allmendinger, wheel on fire."

The signals grow then wane
as exit signs and billboards press
then disappear inside the bright
corn syrup blur
                    where everything
feels dizzied toward a promised future.

Here though (wherever here may be)
only white noise now.
                        And her last night.
Her voice around our clutch
of friends half lacquered on lawn chairs.
"From when I was eight I had to suck it up.

When Mom was sick I cooked our meals.
I never questioned this arrangement.
People kept saying pray. Just pray.
And when she died
                    Kathleen and I got tested.
The results were clear:
both of us carry the disease.
I left the seminary.
                Life was a sinkhole
and I was wild and straggling
and one night
I woke up in a mansion naked.
No one had, you know. I was fine.
Just walking through this mansion naked."

Box stores and crosses on the hills.
An Appaloosa shakes her mane against the purple
mountains tumbling south.
Reverend Billy shouts
"some seeds fall down in thorns and thorns grow up and . . ."
Shadows of the summits blue
across the stream of cars
still streaked with orange.
It feels so close:
that deepest human space
as she described it.
"From the window I could see
neon I knew was Bourbon Street.
My hands grasped air
then tables and mantles.
At the end of a corridor stood a woman.

And she was beautiful.
Everything glistened: curious and living and
I walked
      by catching myself while falling."

LETTER FROM OHIO

The green so green it must be chemical.
Faint drift of charcoal smoke. Rock radio.
The pink azaleas thrusting at the blue.
And all the same desires come crashing back:
incredible X-ed out scenes and afterward
the whoosh of traffic surf, our bodies bathed
in the whole sweep of towers and freeways and
meadows of blanket flowers. I want it all:
heat puddle in the chest, moments like handfuls
of honeycomb, split, dribbling. . . . Enough.
We've lived apart for weeks now and your voice
cracks from the cell reception, hums and dips
and breaks for seconds, as evening peaks to orange
in the sycamores, and the need to see you stretches
into the days that follow: stray lifetime spent
in office rooms and parks and station halls
as they fall to the curve of earth, the ocean.

CAR RADIO NEAR CLEVELAND NEAR DAWN

Ambient whine and fuzz
                   with a bass drum
and ride on top.
             And then the crunching sound
of plainsong synthesized to techno hum.
And then that voice unbound.

And even through melancholic murk
(some tongue-pierced Hildegard von Bingen spent
from rasping
            over percussion gone berserk)

her voice is elegant:
her torn soprano
             curls and slips the words
above the tremor dragging them back down

as fields of pavement jitter past and birds
circle in slant sun.

Like this it comes. Before the singing fades
(and the band's name) a drizzle of heat stirs
in the chest.
          An imprint of cascades
along the flood of years:

apart but constant
                    they come as scattered
patches where all around us bursts alive.

Right here now.
                    Maples. Flecked brick. Some tattered
sign for a blood drive.

1995: THE SAWTOOTHS

Out of the pooled abstractions that still tell
how I felt that evening but not what

this memory returns I almost feel:
my ankles cold as river stones, my feet

balanced on river stones: bent back to cast
the line upstream, as almost amused she sat

on the car hood drinking beer and the last
specked rays of pink and yellow sank in slats

through dripping aspen groves. And I remember
later, alone: silt on my bare feet

pressing the clutch and gas, I watched the embers
not fireflies as I guessed but running lights

descending the Sawtooths, once the home
of the Shoshone (whom history calls

the Snake) toward towns with names too blunt for poems:
toward Lovelock and Dodge City and Twin Falls.

CHICAGO: THE CONGRESS PLAZA

Under crackling paint where the ballroom
opens to alcoves
he loosens his tie and winces.

"So Larissa threw my suitcase
down the stairs and our kids were watching."

Shimmer of ormolu from ceiling coffers.
Someone shouts
"God O God" to blues in the bar.

The whole hotel could be one
resonant chambered
temple of supplicants:

all the cell-phone signals
spidering air with bargains and blandishments
complaints and cries

becoming what . . . one primal invocation?

———

"Mother of memories
                         love that burns in love
who grants me pleasure and
makes me work

remind me of your touch:

first coolness of the coming dark.

Mother of memories
                          love that burns in love."

———

Sloshed babble.
But inside the din
his moan of bare appeal.
"I did addiction therapy
there in Mississippi
same as Tiger Woods.
But here I am and man I have this
lioness waiting in my room."

As if whatever god of our bloodstream
reared up in all the Robber Baron rococo:

all cover of desire peels away.

Like greed revealing an original need:
an urge that sends the Doppler slur of semis
hurtling west on 94

and the voices spidering:

———

"I've seen the past.

My mouth against your thighs
since only on your body
on your neck and clavicles
breast and heartbeat
could I see my past.

These words
faint scents
          time out of time.

These will return
as we have known them. As the sun
returns as sacrament from ocean.

These words
faint scents
          time out of time."

"Someone should strap a muzzle on me
                              tie me down.
I don't know how to bear myself.

Don't know what medicine . . ."

          ——

At dawn a bluish wash
                    sporadic car horns and
everything is
emptiness

till dollied up the lobby by invisible feet
and dribbling light

                squibs on the marble

comes the enormous cube

of crates of milk.

SALT WATER

I.

The shattered volumes of it: walls of blue
fluming as fast as winds. The sheer corrosive
cleanse of it: how insistently it sleeks

down through the mind.
                              Not even on the beach
but driving with dune grass at the roadside

these days when home's gone relative (a room and
cell phone . . . passcodes)
                              all that neural simmer
of wired voices
                    crying "money money money"
shreds to a bare shimmer of white fire:

"desire without an object of desire."

And the world comes all at once. Me sitting here
pinching your picture
                         while fireflies and
cars and maple branches spill to the water's

cycle of smash and pull. And still stand still.

II.

You close your eyes and arteries flash back.
The way the office towers dissolve at dark
to lucent cubes: encrusting, chitinous.
So much money pulsed to code in the ether.

Sometimes the sluicing rush is gorgeous. Sometimes
it seems inhuman pummel: nowhere to hold
and build and no continuing dwelling.

Only the roar that comes so many nights
near sleep. The static drub
                              the erratic horns
and sirens fade from: huge and tremulous
as ocean. If only then, all connection
feels possible again: another's heat

and breath and laughter:
                          barely knowable soul
swift as an eel escaping the slit mesh.

III.

Confessor. Mother. Father. Ghost. The who
you talk to when you're talking to yourself.
The ocean is one version. Gray green in
sawtooth petals
                  all it meets it swallows.

Such pure abandon: it must be what flows
beneath those little mercies when the nerves
give in to sleep, orgasm, even pissing.

Or the instinctual stream of "Jesus! Jesus!"
swims free for moments
                              and it feels like full
release, full trust: as if one listener

absorbed the whole riptide of consciousness.
As if the vacuum pull
                              beneath the blue
slide to the eel-grass ledges and drop-offs

were sentient. Were more than emptiness.

IV.

The scalloped cliffs of Matsushima shine
in this hotel in silk-screen reproduction.

Sliced by the long horizon past Sendai
the sky and ocean mirror, spiraled by breakers.

The way apart from you I picture you:
conjuring moistened lips
                              you gently pinch
then thinking
                    what would it be like to live

inside you, be you: sway of your swift walk
and thrown-back hair, your stuck then wending speech.

And no: it all grows nebulous, like gauze.

Aerial shot . . . night highways wiring
the littoral.
    That animate dark is all.

That space between us.
      Constant. Scintillant.

The water hisses, draining off the sand.

CUYAHOGA COUNTY: SMOKE

As in her throat
a film of ash
blends to body heat
and she thinks   "red brick"
and thinks what usual wrecks
her friends became as
ministers whispered down their ears
and feels on basement couches
chasmed to marriages
of tract homes and Waffle Houses

———

or they vanished
               horse in the veins
nuzzling the wild nasturtiums

———

"God!"
       as she inhales again
and stubs below her easel
she catches
         round her thigh
the blue heron tattoo
blue talisman she took
because   "no different from anyone

I need my flight from hurt"

— ——

and breathes out
                    feeling

"cobalt to bruise the line here.

Yup"   and the red still burns.

for Nicole Robinson

1986: RECURRING DREAM

The dream was that the wilderness snaked up
against the house. Except the wilderness
   was the inside. Which meant inside the house
     was the outside.
                    And all that slipped between
were sounds: not howls of wolves or leopard snarls
   but a dendritic crackle of voices breaking
past the dark boughs:
                  "No, Senator, I don't recall.
The documents were shredded. Colonel North . . ."

Sentences arabesqued round secrecies
   they both denied and by denying blurted:

"Touch me. Yes touch me there. Not there not there."

Behind the trees, the voices lived inside
their shadow government of urge and bright
enticement.
         They were realer than real life.
In snatches through the branches (underwater
   glitter of midnight grids, like that stock shot
down from Mulholland Drive) their secret world
   hovered in glamour.
                But stepping past the trees
never was entrance to a shining center.

Only fluorescent glare and scraps of speech:
   "Mistakes were made. But."
                          "Yes. Oh yes, oh yes."

Then blankness.
                 Then the sun flowed in and clung
   in the curtains
          and glowed across the floor
  and nightstand and your little radio.

DAUGHTER

Following me with my same eyes
her own become two animals

lamb or tiger
I can't tell but

follow inside
                webbed liquid trembling

flashes of my mother
how many years ago   cream skin   forsythia

now TV sputter

"Korengal Valley fire fight . . . Keystone XL Pipeline"
and we hold between us

this quickened

pulse which
                planted in the chest
would make the barest rising syllable

or printed on the world
a luminous   billow of slipstream ruffling to air

1986: THE COURT

Behind our house, although the front was kept
sprinkled and cut, a bramble jungle swept
   down to the vague edge of the property.
     A staircase teetered from the basement door
   and disappeared in briars. It felt to me
     like ugliness. And also weird allure.
Scratched from the tangle, when you reached the end
there was a fence, but only to suspend
   the vines: a hole was ripped in the chain-link
     and opened on a tennis court. Who knows
   how long it lay abandoned. Arrowing slink
     of a garter snake or squawking of some crows.
And there it stood. And I could disappear:
free from the whiplash of that house. That year
   time had a ragged, wavelike undertone.
     My father lived with us again, then didn't.
   Life happened all together, then alone.
     To stomp and shriek and sing and cower, hidden
there on the crumbling court, or even lie
on its cracked clay and watch that square of sky
   like a TV . . . made everything, the gleams
     of rage and happiness, of feral love
   and loneliness, dissolve to jabbering streams
     my hideout floated at the center of.
And I brought others also. I can see
Jason and Lee and Karen crouch with me

coughing on ripped-off cigarettes. Our hair
    almost translucent in the sun, our faces
brimming with sun, we are wholly elsewhere:
    sliced from all time that this one time erases.
The home above, its breaking, shines both clear
and blotched in memory. A purple smear
    of evening rooms and then, slow-mo, a shot
        of screams and smashing glass. The crumbling court
stays, though, as if the details I forgot
        moldered around the edges for support:
the chain-link and its canopy of green
burn to a yellow scribble, while a sheen
    of skin remains there, held against the pull
        of all outside. The netted glimmers leak
across us. Only fragments stand out full:
    lips moist in sunlight opening to speak.

VILLA SCIARRA: AZALEAS

The veins inside the petals overlap
then separate
with such
exactitude.
              The petals wrap
in so smooth-cinched a fit.
Brimming toward touch

the anthers sparkle yellow at the tips.
And the glow
one bead
of nectar holds
                  before it slips
to darker green below . . .
where does it lead:

this pointless staring? How about this day?
If life would just remain
like art.
But months and years
                        bear their array
of happiness or pain
then blur apart.

Tonight on streets beneath the Gianicolo
the staggered flood
will mesh
and tear
             and pull us to its flow.
Craving for dope or food.
For cash or flesh.

Such raw pursuit: as if each person knew
all along
that we burn
inside our lives
                 our whole lives through
and walk inside the throng
and don't return.

And spring still does its spring thing everywhere.
Clouds spiraling
past towers
back in America.
                 Or glare
sleeving an airplane wing.
Or these flowers.

If there's a pattern that a life weaves
it must be fierce
as this old
explosion of petals
                     off the leaves.
Whatever moments pierce
through time and hold

must hang together ragged. Thin membranes
so finely spun
they spill
upward through air:
                their veins
not yet invisible
in the downpouring sun.

ROME

The metal center of the ceiling fan
reflected me: my bare diminutive
cut off from rage and dread, from any plan
I clutched. It told me here is where you live.
Outside, the city wore its walls like masks.
Its famous river pouring green. The young
and almost young in sharp perfumes and musks.
Glow sticks for sale. The Hang Seng numbers, strung
streaming along plate glass. The grid flowed on
and I was part, and nothing was absolute.
The metal center of the ceiling fan
reflected me, my sweating brightness. Brute
blunt spot I was, in being, not desire:
like tigers or the moon or lemon trees
surrendering their presence to the air.
The weightlessness was nothing you could seize.
It meant that you were small and "you" meant me
and her and him. But each was separate:
as if each harbored some unceasing plea.
The way, each fall, new knockout bodies fit
inside the same outlasting billboard space:
I knew my life would disappear from there:
the way the waves of crowds and cars efface
waves—and the cool of being rinsed clear
would vanish. Even then, this trembling core

of white heat (my fear my craving) pooled
and swiveled down. Except it now felt more
like fire—here was where all life was fueled.
The need to fly from need, break wholly out
still pulsed from all the usual broil of feeling
walking past walls, or roses, or a pig snout
hung in a window, scarlet streaks congealing.

OVER GREENLAND: FLIGHT 107

A current
like a noise machine through sleep.

Blue lichen fields.
Mossed boulders.

Waking up
to ice cubes cracking in a plastic cup

and voices
         ("awesome for the Hong Kong branch"

"well, most of all we miss our daughter . . .")

still I see that
         granite trail
where runnels spill

from some bare misted summit like a source.

Whatever sense this dream might make to others

and whatever when they wake
they also have been dreaming

(Lago di Como
and the Baroness   her blue bikini

or herds of antelope

roaming the cubicles in Pocatello)

still: this aluminum vessel
holds it all

and if there is no towering sublime
where everything comes clear

(no final climb through cloud like some old Bible illustration)

how could that ever stop the current flowing
out of the glass at JFK

skin glowing
                plum and peach as we

walk inside the sun.

BLUE FIGURE, DOGU PERIOD

He stiffened a little on the treadmill
and gripped the handles while he tracked the screen.
The picture was a camera crew. Their cameras
shouldered, they shimmied down a pile of rubble
left where the risen ocean clobbered homes.

A surge behind his watching as he watched
the ash reveal a skateboard, overturned.
The wheels collected tiny snowflake domes.
Maybe because full blast in the ear buds
Radiohead's "Weird Fishes" rose and flashed on

breakers of alto cries and arpeggios
or maybe because the captions, lagging, spelled
"leaking reactor core" as the camera panned
once more to the slag heap . . . whatever reason:
far as the stars and right in front of him

sheer being shone there, in the light of catastrophe
that edged the streams of fleeing families
and lingered even past the commercial babble
("Ultimate Connectivity for Less")
as the treadmill beeped and shuddered to "Cool Down"

and he remembered: in the locker room
he'd need to wipe his antifungal cream
around his torso, neck, as far around
his back as he could reach, then need to wait
ten minutes with his skin that smeary blue and

hunch on the bench, hang tight, embarrassment
tremoring through him like dismay or fear
whose cause had fogged, forgotten. He would wave
to others passing there. Would tap his chest:
"Hey man. I'm blue today. I guess I'm blue."

ELEGY WITH TELEVISION

I.

A clearing in the pines and snow swept
around a square of earth. Our steaming breath.
The way one window frame from the condos
imprinted down my eye because we all were
weeping and everything went streaked then vivid.
Kneeling to the patch of Astroturf
to scatter my handful of soil . . . it hit:
the sobbing like a plunge to a reservoir
of heat beneath the rib cage—submerged
then up, then plunged again—was not because
her fingers in her wedding photograph
twisting to clip her veil (so delicate)
were ash: she still was there. Her Auntie Wisdom
simper imploring us "Oh, please enough"
beneath her own wet eyes was palpable
as snow on gravel. Only looking up
from the ground now: where to find her? Where render
this sheerest feeling toward her?
                                    In her ranch house
wedged to a wicker cabinet, her TV
fluttered above me all the afternoons
my parents dropped me there. And the stories
up on the screen. And the crinkle of banked fire
her old retriever snored beneath. So close

to permanence: the warmth she carried round her
loomed as an element my life could enter.

Over us now the window frame ballooned.
It showered blue and silver, and was gone.
We walked the trampled path behind the priest
back to the idling purr of the warm cars.

II.

I'm reading scholarship about TV.
The writer claims it streams two ways at once.
It pours the aggregate inside the home
so people of every race and cheetahs
in the Okavango, sales on furniture
and faces of refugees (some flattened ghost
at least in digital particulate)
all overflow the limits of the place
we're watching from. It also filters out.
The spectacles of public life now shrink
to the console. And what gets blinkered off
turns easier for power to control.

I've drifted from the theories. But a trace
of networks cinching us between what screens
we're allowed to see—from the side porch, June heat
still thick at evening: the street lights strung
in forced perspective could be bastions, driven
into whatever's out there as inside
(shivers branching the gut) white heat coils down.

Long corridors. A whiff of disinfectant.
The complex she endured the last ten years
until she swallowed the pills she stashed (how long?)
for when it came to this. But came to what?
The feeling she was losing the mind she used
to feel she was losing it? The corridors
like tunnels of pastels, kitsch wreaths, her neighbors
glaring from neighbor masks? But she was lucid.

Just days before, her voice on the receiver
growling about "that fool" the President.

Her congregation, though the priest at last
ran interference, wanted to refuse
her burial rites: as if the universe blared rules
as firm as walls and all beyond were night.

And yet her plot: the cube with its five sides
of glinting earth and one of open air
could be an emblem of the self, the recessed
volume displaying all it also hides.

Corrections penciled on the article
she almost finished. And the paper whites
leaked their sweet ammoniac reek
among the slats of sun and the dust whirl.

III.

A girl in Kansas on a snow-swept hill
where the Command and General Staff School
skirts the Missouri, you crouched to aim your sled.

And stopped.
                    Figures were circling a black tree.
Two soldiers lifted a stretcher. It was
Elizabeth Andrus who had, you remembered, "eyes
like coffee beans." By morning, word spread
round Leavenworth. She died. A ruptured spleen.

The funeral parlor's candelabras wavererd
over the coffin: short, mahogany.
Her face a slice of moon in the brown air
too sweet from lilies. And the gladiolas
scissoring everywhere.
                    These entrances
of others in your life, however long
they stay, and then their disappearances:
I want to ask you is this all, this press
of faces more and more eclipsed to gray
and no great pattern holding us together?

I hear your voice: "I still *hate* gladiolas!"

IV.

Then two years after the memorial.
LaGuardia. Morning dark on the plate glass.
My nerves all tangle and snap from no sleep.
Channeling up the ramp one face was
so familiar. Daniel? Dan? David?
His freckled brow imprinted and decades
broke off to cubes, were sectioned air our bodies
plummet inside . . . and Dan or Donald turned.
I didn't know him. But the feeling comes
even weeks later now. Paco Rabanne
and phosphorescent phones. An earbud wire
and lilac muumuu. Laurie? Lindsay? Lorraine?

Each profile glowed distinct and yet a tincture
pooled in the eyes: one molten soul inside
the finite ways skin rides the bone and bone
pulls skin across it.
                        On the hanging screens
the soldiers glowed night vision google green.
Machine guns. And the anchor's face shellacked
with decency:
                        as if the surface of the world
were cover up: those pixilated features
slackening back to sympathetic grimace
masked an invisible force held static on each
screen through the tapering terminal.

The window frame above her funeral
glistened with the same insinuation:
each smallest particle of memory

(her fingers liver-spotted on a plastic cup
enameled with daisies)
                              could be preserved

and even her suicide appeared her slicing
through her expected slow occlusion to this
shiver of both arrival and departure

where any other pair of eyes meets yours
in long-remembered but till now forgotten
silent, articulate, animal glimmers.

And it snapped off. No world behind the world.
Only the forced perspective corridor.

Only the crawl of numbers on the screens.

And hours later, like a dream but clear:
solidity of strapped-in bodies. Snoring.

Out the window near Wichita, blue lines
of streetlights ascended from the snow.

VERMONT: BLOOD BROOK

Glug then sluice for vowels.
Rock ladders for consonants.
Out of the mountain it curls
and glints
        past the mechanic shop
scrap heap then tennis courts

and widens to a band
of silver that suspends

brook trout no longer than a hand.

My center of the world.
Source and burial ground
and only what it is.

I would be a liar
to call them
        shepherd voices
babbling.
      But they do:

crossing the concrete
under a trestle bridge
sprayed with graffiti and

ailanthus leaves

        they call me

video trance boy   seed packet.

You who are not us and will be.

We who pour ourselves

out of ourselves forever.

AFTER BAUDELAIRE: "I HAVE NOT FORGOTTEN . . ."

I have not forgotten, at the town
limits, that quiet house we used to own.
How there in plaster my own decrepit Venus
leaning through ivy garlanding the trellis
shone naked in the light, when sunset felt
whole hours long: gold in a slow melt
across the glass, sun glowed then like an eye
tracking us through curious sky
as we silently ate, as light flowed in
and, generously, clung to the muslin.

LOS ANGELES RIVER

The concrete channel for flood control
has nothing to control today
but litter. Is it even wet

down there? Some little puddles
shimmer around the punk rock weeds.
Or else the shimmer's heat mirage.

This city deals in heat mirage.
Dreams of arrival as a star
streaming through canyon parties. Dreams

of pink Camaro flames released
to flare from El Centro checkpoint.
Right here could be where dreams end up:

film scattered on a concrete river.
Some animal must have a home
there in the weeds, some creature soul

(probably rabid) must make do there
scavenging claw to fang: some urge
constant as blood or breath must circle

up from the faintest synapse fire
to begin again again
from way down make it hurt abandon.

VERMONT: GILE MOUNTAIN

Even that current rapid in the brain
like a digital signal cheeping "where
where where" damps down in the broil of noon.

Below, the ponds and metal rooftops blur
to streaks. And this need, to peel the bright veneer
from the world, and walk inside, and feel my life

crucial as plotline, seems to disappear.
The aspens sizzle. Towers of loosestrife
shiver with flies. Elsewhere a satellite

opens its shutter, clicks on freeways and fields.
Elsewhere demonstrators, chanting, fight
to hold ground against the encroaching shields.

Elsewhere a grizzly blinks at the sun motes.
And all that shimmering merge dissolves now. Here
the world is oak leaf, stillness, blue. It floats

in the heat, goes liquid at the edges, clear.
That digital tremor, that hard-wired burning
that signals just beyond beyond beyond

real life lies waiting: even its returning
now is no distraction but feels bound
to fierce calm. The granite ledges glare

beneath the pine boughs, quaver, and the heart
beats out, right now, one thing with others here:
shot through with light and natural and a part.

INDY CAR

The way in the Best Buy
this moment as flat screens
flash like an insect eye
my son stands mesmerized
by close-ups of a driver
strapped to a cockpit
(the world becomes a narrow
river along his visor)
and Jack is fully in it
begging me "stay no stay
no Daddy just a minute"
till sliding glass
opens and here we are
with waves of sun
pooling on car hoods
and the moaned appeals:
"can we go to Petco?
not to buy animals
just see them . . ."
                    the present tense
holding us in the whole
fissuring gorgeous flood
of all I can't control
or understand or keep
we ride together silent
now and now discussing

what if giraffes stampeded
down the road beside us
why do people die
and hey: by the monkey bars
and classroom windows dark
for summer: those floating spots
like miniature clouds or ghosts
are fruit from the cottonwoods.

DANDELIONS

After the cling of roots and then the "pock"
when they gave way
                   the recoil up the hand
      was a small shock
of emptiness beginning to expand.

Milk frothing from the stems. Leaves inky green
and spiked.
            Like blissed-out childhood play
      turned mean
they snarled in tangled curls on the driveway.

It happens still. The desolating falling
shudder inside
              and then our neighborhood
      is only sprawling
loops, like the patterns eaten on driftwood:

even the home where we grew up (its smell
of lingering
             wood smoke and bacon grease)
      falls to a shell
of lath and paper. But this strange release

follows, this pure luxuriance to feel
the pull of dirt
                    again: sense mist uncurling
            to reveal
no architecture hidden behind the world

except the stories that we make unfolding:
as if our sole real power
                            were the power
                of children holding
this flower that is a weed that is a flower.

NOTES

The epigraph is taken from Herman Melville's *Moby-Dick; or, The Whale.*

"Salt Water (I)": The line in quotation comes from Wallace Stevens's "Chaos in Motion and Not in Motion."

"Chicago: The Congress Plaza": Lines from this poem translate passages from Baudelaire's "Le Balcon."

"Letter from Ohio": Lines from this poem were set to music by Lisa Bielawa in her "Graffiti d'Amante."

"Concourse C": Lines from this poem translate Anglo-Saxon riddles spoken by the wind. The author's full translation appears in *The Word Exchange*, ed. Greg Delanty and Michael Matto (New York: W. W. Norton, 2010).